CHECKERBOARD HOW-TO LIBRARY

COOL ART

COOL DRAWING

THE ART OF CREATIVITY FOR KIDS!

ANDERS HANSON

ABDO
Publishing Company

CONTENTS

Published by ABDO Publishing Company, 8000 West 78th Street, Edina, Minnesota 55439.

Copyright © 2009 by Abdo Consulting Group, Inc. International copyrights reserved in all countries.

No part of this book may be reproduced in any form without written permission from the publisher. The Checkerboard Library™ is a trademark and logo of ABDO Publishing Company.

Printed in the United States.

Editor: Pam Price

Series Concept: Nancy Tuminelly

Cover and Interior Design: Anders Hanson, Mighty Media

Photo Credits: Anders Hanson, Shutterstock

Library of Congress Cataloging-in-Publication Data

Hanson, Anders, 1980-

Cool drawing : the art of creativity for kids / Anders Hanson.

p. cm. -- (Cool art)

Includes bibliographical references and index.

ISBN 978-1-60453-142-8 (alk. paper)

1. Drawing--Technique--Juvenile literature. I. Title.

NC655.H37 2008

741.2--dc22

2008008642

Get the Picture!

When a step number in an activity has a colored circle around it, look for the picture that goes with it. The picture's border will be the same color as the circle.

2   ·········➤

THE ART OF creativity

You Are Creative

Being creative is all about using your imagination to make new things. Coming up with new ideas and bringing them to life is part of being human. Everybody is creative! Creative thinking takes time and practice. But that's okay, because being creative is a lot of fun!

Calling All Artists

Maybe you believe that you aren't good at art. Maybe you have some skills that you want to improve. The purpose of this book is to help you develop your visual creativity. Remember that your artistic skills improve every time you make art. The activities in this book can help you become the creative artist you want to be!

Creativity Tips

- Stay positive.
- There is no wrong way to be creative.
- Allow yourself to make mistakes.
- Tracing isn't cheating.
- Practice, practice, practice.
- Be patient.
- Have fun!

Drawing IS COOL!

Drawing is still basically the same as it has been since prehistoric times. It brings together man and the world. It lives through magic. —Keith Haring

What Is Drawing?

Drawing is making marks on a surface to communicate ideas or feelings.

The earliest known drawings were made on the walls of caves with burnt sticks. Thousands of years later, paper was invented. This gave artists a more plentiful and consistent surface to draw on.

Drawing tools developed as well. Artists made brushes from animal hair. They sharpened sticks and feathers and dipped them in ink to create pens. They rubbed soft metals, such as lead and silver, and iron-rich chalks onto paper.

Today's tools are more advanced, but the goal of drawing is still communication. Drawing is a language we can all use and understand, no matter where we come from.

Prehistoric Drawing

Before there was written language, there was drawing. **Archaeologists** have found hundreds of drawings of animals and people at Chauvet Cave in France. Early artists made these cave drawings about 30,000 years ago!

The drawings tell stories about both their subjects and the people who drew them. They tell us of artists who understood their world. These artists wanted to share their knowledge and experiences. They accomplished that through drawing.

The Value of Drawing

Drawing is often thought of as the foundation of the visual arts. Before artists begin new works, they often make many quick sketches of what it might look like. These drawings help artists plan their projects. They also help them visualize which ideas will be more successful than others.

When he was 73, the great Japanese artist Hokusai wrote about drawing. He discussed what he had learned during nearly 60 years of practicing art. And, he discussed what he expected to learn in coming decades. He ended by saying, "When I am 110, everything I do, be it a dot or a line, will be alive."

It's clear that drawing can take a lifetime to learn. Even the great Hokusai believed he still had much to learn after 60 years of drawing!

SELF PORTRAIT AS AN OLD MAN — HOKUSAI

Learning to Draw

Great artists are not always satisfied with their work. Part of what makes them great is that they are always trying to get better. You don't need to be good at drawing now to become a great artist. You just need the desire to learn and become better!

Be patient with yourself. Changes won't happen overnight. When you do a drawing you don't like, don't throw it out. Save it so you can look back later and see how much you've improved! Have **confidence** in yourself. You can do anything you set your mind to!

Don't Be a Judge!

When discussing a drawing, avoid using the words listed below. They offer judgments without saying much about the character of the work. Instead, look at how the artist used composition and **techniques**. Try to understand what the artist was trying to achieve. See pages 8 through 15 to read about these elements.

- good
- bad
- right
- wrong
- silly
- stupid

5

TOOLS OF THE TRADE

PENCILS

THIN CHARCOAL

MEDIUM CHARCOAL

THICK CHARCOAL

PENS

CHARCOAL PENCILS

WHITE PENCIL

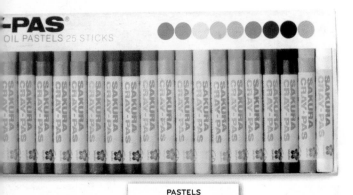

PASTELS

WHITE ERASER

KNEADED ERASER

BLENDING TOOLS

Each activity in this book has a list of the tools and materials you need. When you come across a tool you don't know, turn back to these pages. You can find most of these items at your local art store.

FLAT BRUSHES

BLACK INK

ROUND BRUSHES

WATERCOLOR PAPER

WATERCOLORS

MEDIUM-VALUE PAPER

SKETCH BOOK

7

Basic Elements

These are the elements that make up images. All drawings can be described by these key **concepts**.

Point

The point is the most basic element of drawing. Touching a drawing tool to a surface and immediately removing it creates a point.

Line

Connecting two points creates a line. Lines can be straight, angled, or curved. They may be thick or thin. Lines can be hard and rigid or soft and sketchy.

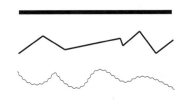

Shape

When lines enclose a space, they create a shape. A shape can be **geometric**, such as a circle or a square, or **irregular**. Shapes may be empty or solid.

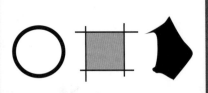

Pattern

Points, lines, and shapes can create a pattern when they repeat in an organized and **predictable** way.

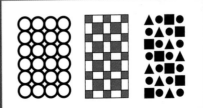

Texture

You can create texture by repeating points, lines, or shapes. Make them so small that you can't easily see the individual elements.

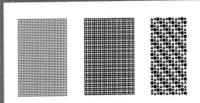

Value

Value describes how light or dark a color is. Lighter objects have little value. Dark objects have a lot of value.

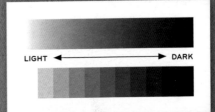

Color

You can make every color by mixing the primary colors. Mixing any two primary colors creates a secondary color.

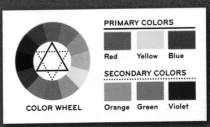

Composition

Bringing together the basic elements to make a work of art is called composition. The following ideas will help you create great compositions!

Focal Point

The focal point is the first thing you see when you look at a drawing. Without a focal point, a drawing may seem **chaotic**.

FOCUSED

UNFOCUSED

Balance

Balance refers to the arrangement of elements in a collage. Evenly spread objects create balance. Objects grouped in one area create an unbalanced composition.

Movement

Movement occurs when things appear to be traveling across a drawing. The image on the left moves like a river. The one on the right feels calm, like a lake.

MOVEMENT

STILLNESS

BALANCED

UNBALANCED

Space

Whenever lines enclose a space, two shapes are made. The shape inside the lines is called positive space. The shape outside the lines is called negative space. When these shapes work well together, the composition is more interesting.

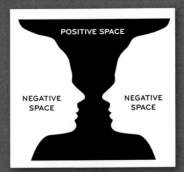

POSITIVE SPACE

NEGATIVE SPACE

NEGATIVE SPACE

Rhythm

Rhythm isn't just for musicians! Artists repeat brushstrokes or shapes to give their work rhythm.

RHYTHMIC LINES

Harmony

When two or more elements in a drawing share **characteristics**, they are in **harmony**. When elements don't have much in common, they are **dissonant**. Characteristics that help create harmony include color, size, and shape.

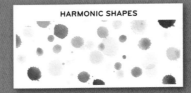

HARMONIC SHAPES

DISSONANT SHAPES

Contrast

Contrast occurs when a work has both extremes of an element. Smooth and rough textures, light and dark values, and large and small shapes are a few examples.

LOW VALUE CONTRAST

HIGH VALUE CONTRAST

Techniques

Artists use various **techniques** to create the elements of a drawing. Pick up a pencil and try these techniques as you read about them.

Expressive Lines

Although a point may be the most basic element, the line is the most useful. A single line can communicate feeling. Look at the different kinds of lines on the right. How do they make you feel?

Hatching

One way to create value is to **hatch**, or to draw many lines going the same direction. Thick lines placed very close together create a dark value. Thin lines placed farther apart make a lighter value.

Crosshatching

Crosshatching is drawing layers of straight lines that are on top of each other but going different directions. Crosshatching creates a grid-like texture.

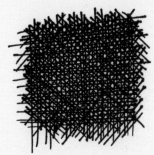

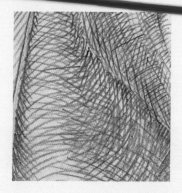

Contour Hatching

In contour hatching, the curve and direction of the lines help define a three-dimensional form. Curved hatching emphasizes the shape of a rounded object better than straight lines would.

Scumbling

Scumbling is another way to create value. Like hatching, scumbling calls for repeating one kind of mark until you achieve the desired value. But, instead of groups of parallel lines, scumbling can involve any type of mark you want! Different kinds of marks result in different textures.

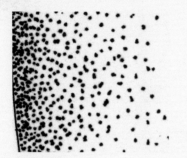

Stippling

Stippling is drawing many points to create value. The closer together the points are, the darker the value. The size and value of the individual points also affect the value of the stippled area.

Smudging

Smudging is a way to blend values. Using a blending tool or a folded paper towel, gently rub or push graphite or charcoal around on the paper. The result is smooth change of value and a flat, even texture.

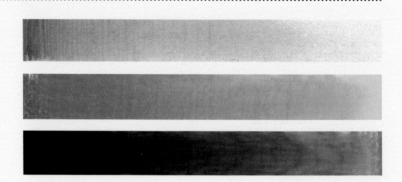

Erasing

Use erasers to correct unwanted pencil or charcoal marks. Press a kneaded eraser onto marks to reduce their impact and value. Use a white eraser to completely remove marks. White erasers have sharp edges, so they are more **accurate**.

Ink Wash

Mix black ink with water to create different values of ink wash. Do the mixing in small paper cups. For light values, mix a small amount of ink into water. For darker values, mix a little water into ink. Use a brush to apply the wash.

Wet-on-Wet

Applying an ink wash to an area that is wet is called wet-on-wet. Wet-on-wet is a fun and unpredictable **technique**. You never know exactly how the washes will mix with each other or **bleed** into surrounding areas. So, it's nearly impossible to control the results!

Dry Brushing

When you dry brush, you dip a brush into watercolor or ink. Then you wipe off the excess moisture before applying the dried brush to the drawing.

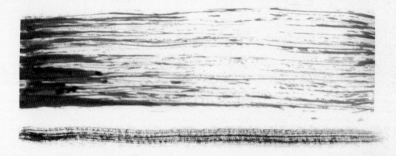

WARM-UP

Put on a tune and draw your favorite music!

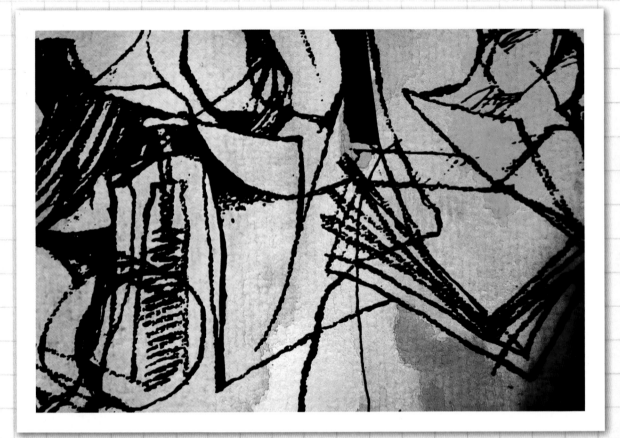

Stuff You'll Need
Sketchpad, pastels, watercolors, brushes

1. Put on a song you like and just listen to it. How does it make you feel? Is it happy and energetic or sad and slow? If it has lyrics, just focus on the sounds and rhythms. After the song is over, get out your sketchpad and drawing tools and find a comfortable space to work.

Tunes to Try

- "A Day in the Life" by the Beatles
- *The Four Seasons* by Antonio Vivaldi
- *The Planets* by Gustav Holst

Setting Up

- Put an extra sheet of paper under your drawing paper. This provides a smoother drawing surface.
- Cover the edges of your paper with artist's tape. This creates a small white border.
- Give yourself enough space to work.
- Place your drawing tools within arm's reach.
- Work in a well-lit area.
- When working with messy materials, such as ink, put down a couple layers of newspaper. The newspaper will catch drips or splatters.

2. Play the song again and begin drawing. Try not to draw anything in particular. Let the sound of the music influence what you are doing. During fast parts of the song you might want to draw quickly. Use your whole arm and make fast, energetic marks. During slower parts, you could draw steadily using mostly your wrist and elbow.

3. Think about movement, balance, space, rhythm, **harmony**, and contrast. How does the music relate to these ideas? For instance, if the music makes you feel uneasy, try making an unbalanced composition. If it has a strong beat, try repeating an element a few times to create rhythm.

4. Does the melody make you think of any colors? If so, add them with pastels or watercolors.

5. When the song is over, stop drawing. If you aren't happy with what the drawing looks like, that's okay. You can always make another one! But remember, it's not supposed to look like anything. The goal is to think creatively and have fun!

MEGA MONTAGE

Get to know contour lines!

Stuff You'll Need

Old magazines, scissors, paper, artist's tape, window with good light, pencils, pens, white eraser, pastels, blending tool

1 Ask an adult for magazines that you can cut up. Look through them to find large, cool images you like. Animals, people, trees, and buildings are a few ideas. Cut out about 10 pages you'd like to make a **montage** with.

2 Turn your drawing paper over. Place a picture facedown on the drawing paper and tape it in place. Turn the paper back over.

3 Can you see the image's light and dark areas through the drawing paper? If not, tape it to a window that gets good light.

4 Look for edges, lines, and sharp **transitions** between light and dark areas. These are called contours. Trace lines over all the contours with a pencil.

5 You now have a contour line drawing! Remove the picture from the back of the paper and repeat steps 2 through 4 with the rest of your images. Try to fill up most of your paper with lines and shapes.

6 Let your contour drawings overlap each other. Interesting and random shapes will appear. Try rotating the images or turning them upside down before you trace them.

7 When you're done, take a look at your composition. Trace over the lines you like best with a thick drawing pen. Try not to trace all the lines from any one object. Instead, look for interesting lines that connect a few objects. If you want to create any new lines, now is the time.

8 Carefully erase all the pencil lines with a white eraser.

9 Now it's time to add some color! Get out your pastels and a blending tool. Color each shape however you'd like. Use the blending tool to make soft **transitions** between colors.

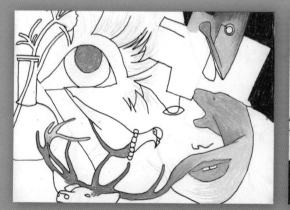

THE BLIND LINE

Practice your powers of observation with a friend!

Stuff You'll Need
Sketchbooks or paper, pens, a partner

Seeing Without Symbols

Symbols are graphics that have been simplified so that they are easy to understand and remember. Symbols are very useful. But when it comes to drawing things we see, symbols only get in the way.

Think about a tree. You know what a tree looks like, right? Try to draw a tree without looking at one. If it looks like one of the symbols below, then you are drawing a symbol of tree.

Actual trees are much more **complicated**. Instead of a circle or a triangle at the top, they have hundreds of branches. The branches twist and turn and end in leaves or needles of all different shapes. What's more, no two trees are alike. So when you want to draw something that looks real, be sure to look at it very carefully.

SYMBOLS ACTUAL SHAPE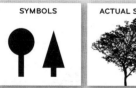

1 Grab a friend or a parent and sit facing each other at a table. Read the rules below before you start.

Rule 1: After you start drawing, don't take your eyes off your partner, especially not to look at your drawing. Really! Don't look at your drawing until you're done!

Rule 2: Once your pen touches the paper, don't lift it off until you're finished. The trick is to avoid jumping from area to area. Start at the center of the face, drawing the eyes, nose, and mouth. Gradually move to the outer edges of the face. Then draw the contours of the hair, neck, body, and clothing.

2 Imagine that your eyes and your pen are directly connected. As you move your eyes along the contours of your partner, move your pen along the drawing surface. Try to draw every curve and angle that your eyes see.

3 When you're finished, take a look at your drawing. It probably won't look a whole lot like your partner. That's okay! The goal of this exercise is to develop a better connection between your eyes and your hand. Drawing what you see, not what you know, is a big step in becoming a better artist.

STILL LIFE

Create lifelike drawings with value!

Preventing Smudging

- If you're right-handed, try starting on the left side of the drawing. For left-handers, begin on the right.
- Put a piece of paper or a paper towel under your drawing hand.
- If these tips don't help, have an adult spray the drawing with workable fixative. After it dries, you can begin drawing again.

Stuff You'll Need
A still life arrangement, black and white charcoal pencils, medium-value colored paper

1. Find three or four interesting objects that look like they'd be fun to draw. Arrange them close together on a table. Make sure you'll still have room to set up your drawing space at the table.

2. You need a strong source of light for this project. If your arrangement isn't getting a lot of light, you'll need a lamp. Ask an adult to help you set up a lamp close by.

3. Choose a colored paper with a medium value. If it's too light or dark, parts of your drawing will not show up well.

4. Start by doing a light contour line sketch with a hard pencil. The objects should fill up most of the paper. Study the still life carefully and use the observational skills you learned in the last activity. But this time, you can look at your paper anytime!

5 Now look for the light areas, or highlights, of the arrangement. With white charcoal, draw the lightest highlights first. Press down firmly to make these areas as white as possible. Then fill in the second-lightest highlights, pressing down a little more softly.

6 Find the dark areas, or shadows, of the still life. Using black charcoal, draw these areas on your paper. Make the darkest areas as black as possible.

7 Don't trace over any of the contour lines you drew. Try to create the illusion of form using only value.

8 You don't need to draw the medium values. The value of the paper should take care of those!

ACTION FIGURES

Learn to draw the human figure!

Stuff You'll Need
Model, watercolor paper, ink wash, brushes

1. In a small paper cup, mix water and ink in equal parts. You won't need more than about a tablespoon of each. Put a couple of layers of newspaper down around your workspace to absorb any splattered ink.

2. Have a friend or parent pose for you. Your model should choose a position that will be comfortable for about five minutes.

3. Choose a medium-sized round brush. Paint the shape of the torso, or midsection, of your model.

4. Paint the shape of the head and the neck on top of the torso.

5. Add the legs and the feet.

6. Paint the arms and the hands.

7. Have your model change to a different pose and repeat steps 3 through 6.

8. Give your model a break! Allow your drawing to fully dry in a safe, flat place.

SELF-PORTRAIT

It's all about you!

Stuff You'll Need

Mirror, paper, pencils, charcoal, blending tool, eraser

1. Carefully study your face in the mirror. Starting with the center of the face, lightly sketch the contour lines. Use the chart on the right to help with the proportions. Your face should fill up most of the page.

2. Look for the darkest areas of your face. The pupils, eye sockets, nostrils, mouth line, hair, and ears are good places to start. Using charcoal, draw the blackest areas as darkly as possible.

3. Draw the medium values using your charcoal stick. You can use a blending tool or a paper towel to smudge and soften areas.

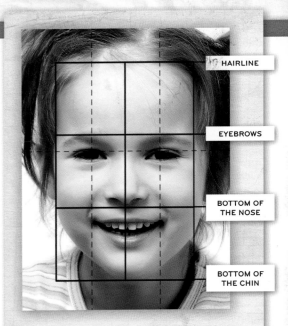

HAIRLINE

EYEBROWS

BOTTOM OF THE NOSE

BOTTOM OF THE CHIN

Facial Proportion

Every face is different. But, following basic rules of proportion can help you create lifelike faces.

- Faces can be divided into thirds. The upper third is from the hairline to the eyebrows. The middle third is from the eyebrows to the bottom of the nose. The lower third is from the bottom of the nose to the bottom of the chin.

- The tops of the ears line up with the centers of the eyes. The bases of the ears line up with the bottom of the nose.

- The centers of the eyes roughly line up with the corners of the mouth.

- The space between the eyes is about the width of one eye.

what's next?

Taking Care of Your Drawings

Drawings are delicate creatures. Storing or treating a drawing improperly could wreck it. Here are a few tips to help keep your drawings in good condition.

- If you have large, loose drawing papers, consider buying an inexpensive cardboard portfolio to keep them in. You can find one at any art store. And, cardboard portfolios actually work better than the expensive leather portfolios!

- Have an adult spray your pencil or charcoal drawings with workable fixative. It's dangerous, so don't use the fixative without supervision.

- Put a sheet of newsprint or an extra sheet of paper between drawings in your portfolio. This will prevent them from rubbing off on one another.

Try Something New!

The activities in this book are just a few examples of fun drawing projects you can do. Once you've completed them all, go back and try some of the projects with different materials or subjects. Try mixing different media in the same drawing. Then make up some projects of your own!

Keeping a Sketchbook

Keeping a small sketchbook and a pencil with you at all times is a great way to improve your drawing skills. Whenever you see something you want to draw, just get your sketchbook. You'll never be bored again!

GLOSSARY

accurate – free of errors.

archaeologist – one who studies the remains of people and activities from ancient times.

bleed – to flow into neighboring areas.

chaotic – of or relating to a state of total confusion.

characteristic – a quality or a feature of something.

complicated – having many related parts.

concept – an idea.

confidence – a feeling of faith in your own abilities.

dissonant – having parts that don't go well together.

geometric – made up of straight lines, circles, and other simple shapes.

harmony – having parts that go well together.

hatch – to draw a series of fine lines close together to create a shading effect.

irregular – lacking symmetry or evenness.

montage – a picture made by combining several different pictures.

predictable – being able to guess the outcome of an event based on reason, experience, or observation.

technique – a method or style in which something is done.

transition – a movement from one style, stage, or form to another.

Web Sites

To learn more about cool art, visit ABDO Publishing Company on the World Wide Web at **www.abdopublishing.com**. Web sites about cool art are featured on our Book Links page. These links are routinely monitored and updated to provide the most current information available.

INDEX